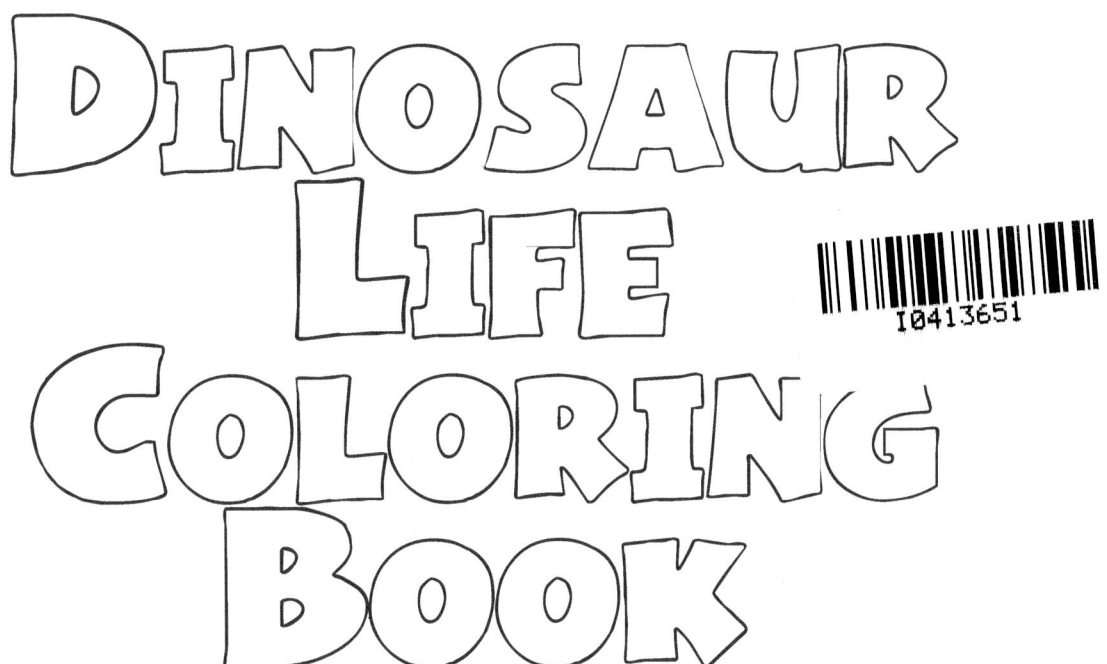

DINOSAUR LIFE COLORING BOOK

BY SUSAN POTTERFIELDS

Copyright © 2016 Susan Potterfields

All rights reserved.

ISBN: 10: 1534839380
ISBN-13: 978-1534839380

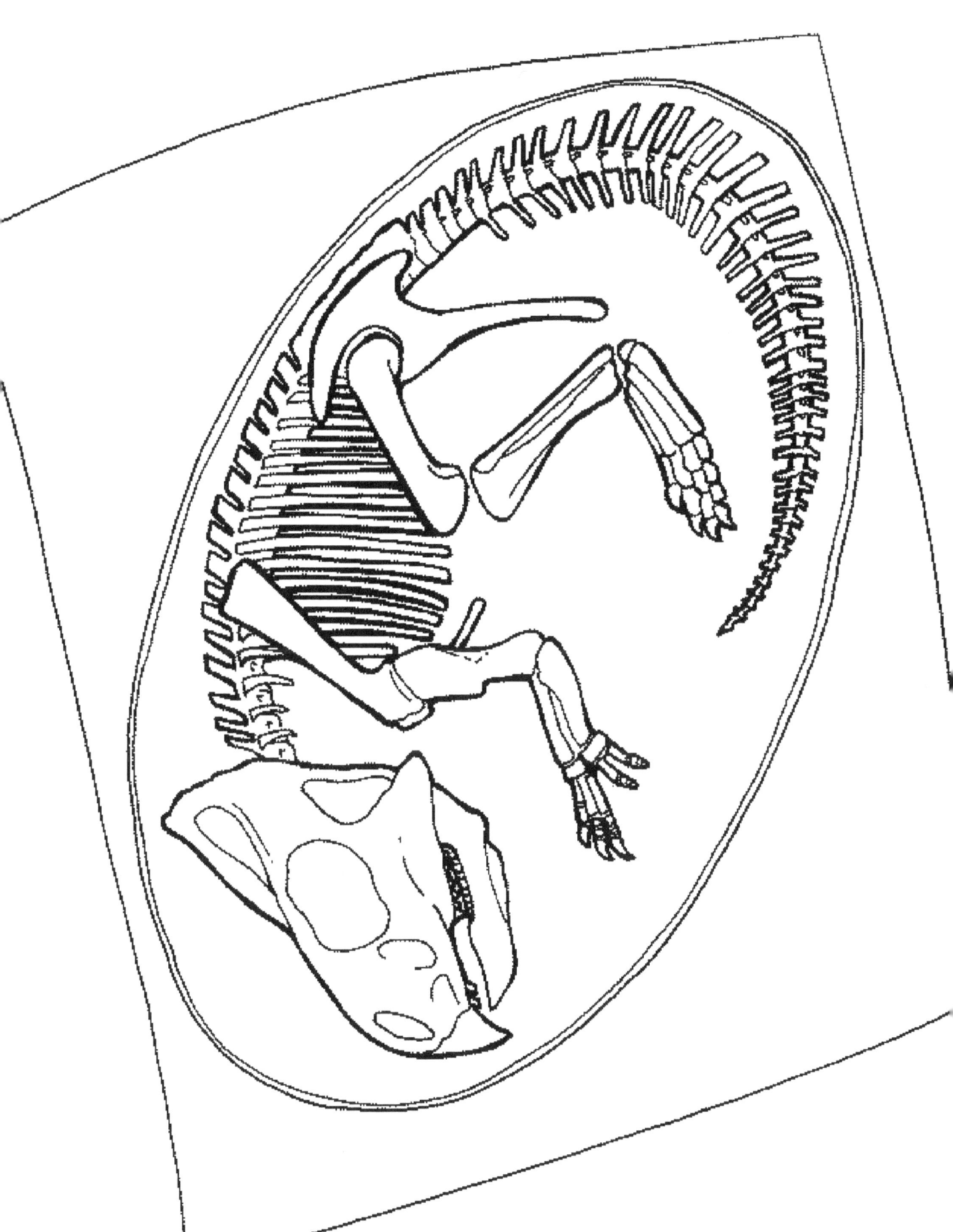

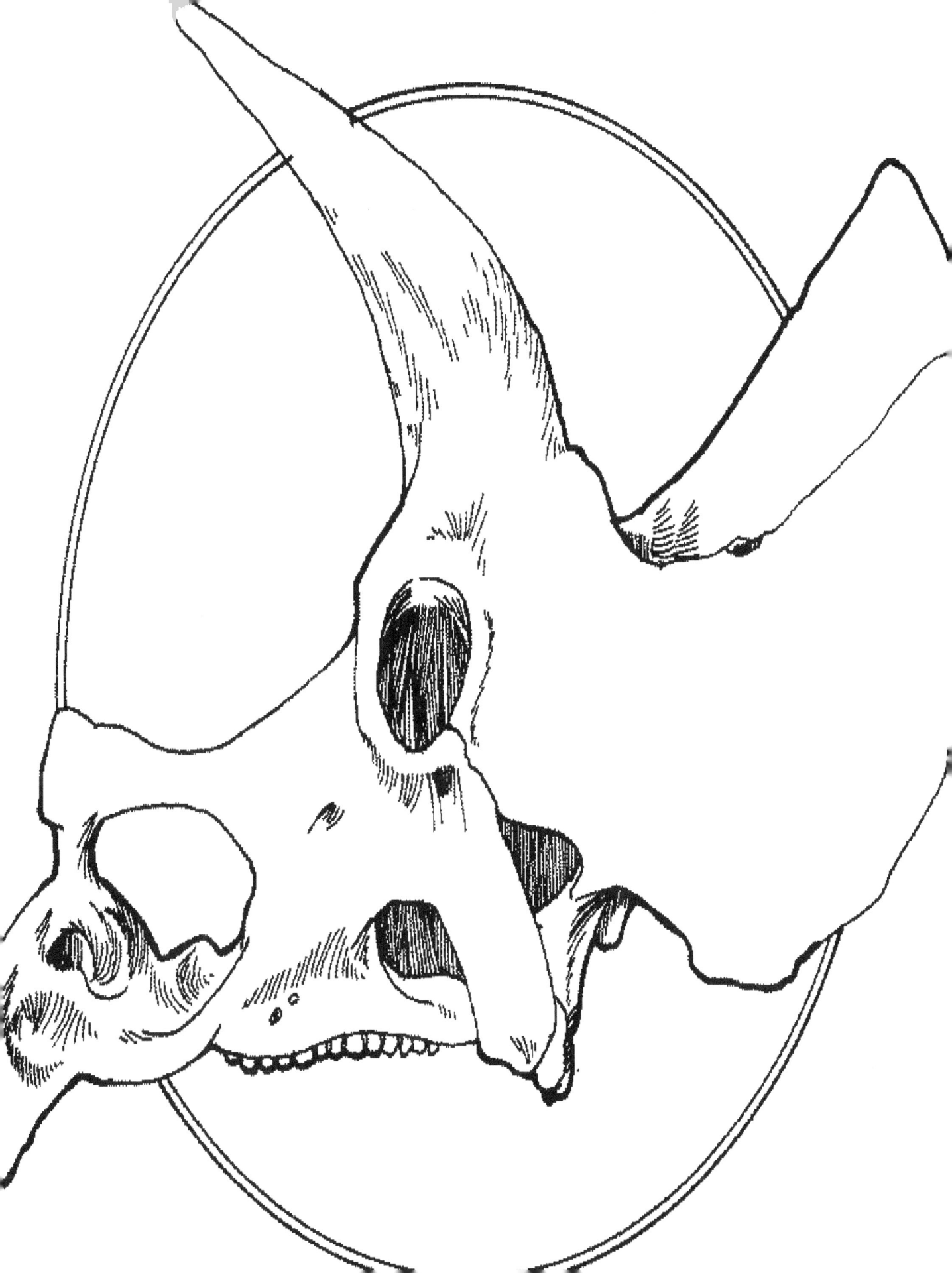

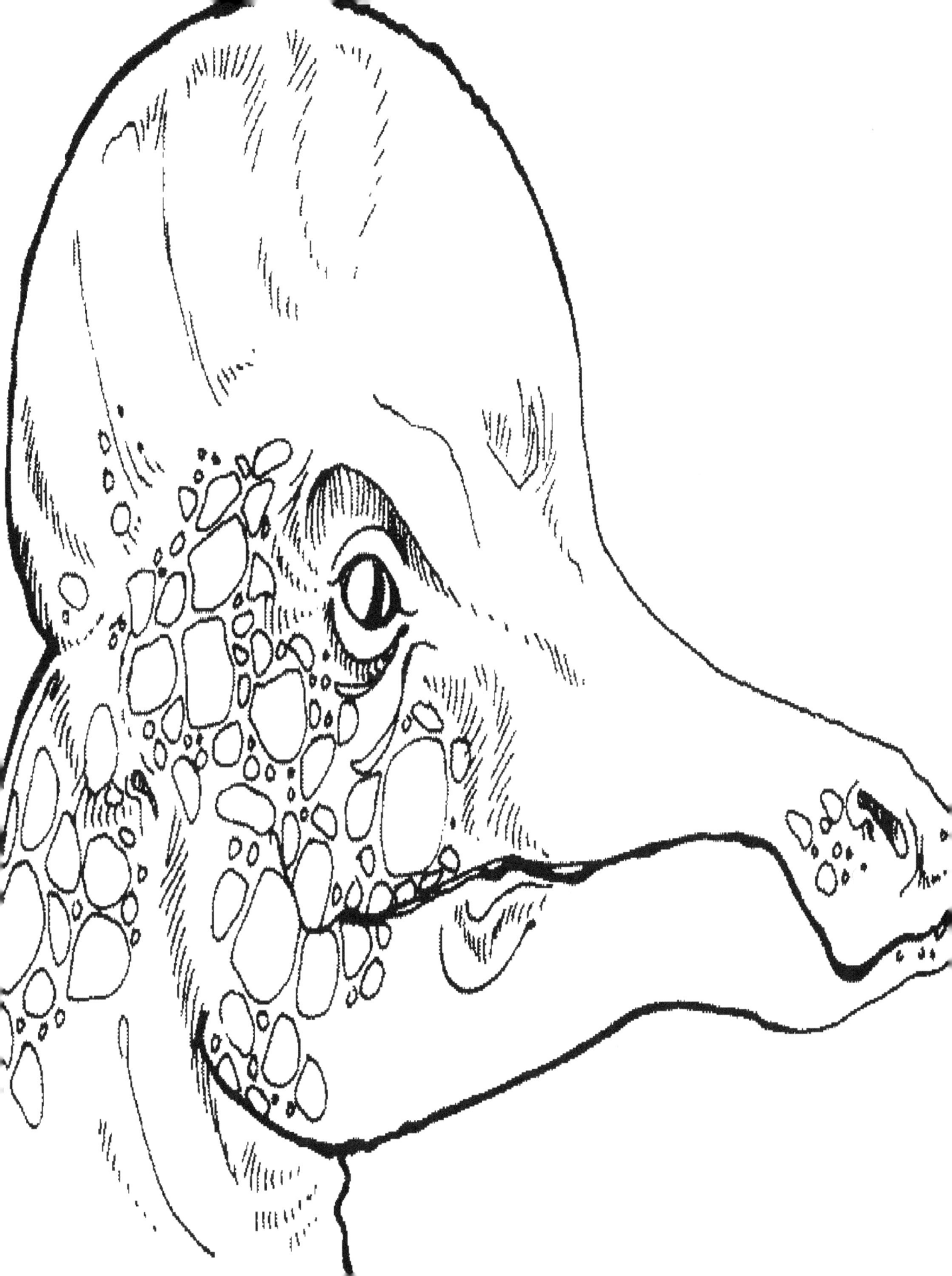

www.ingramcontent.com/pod-product-compliance
Lightning Source LLC
Chambersburg PA
CBHW081119280526
45787CB00007B/2901